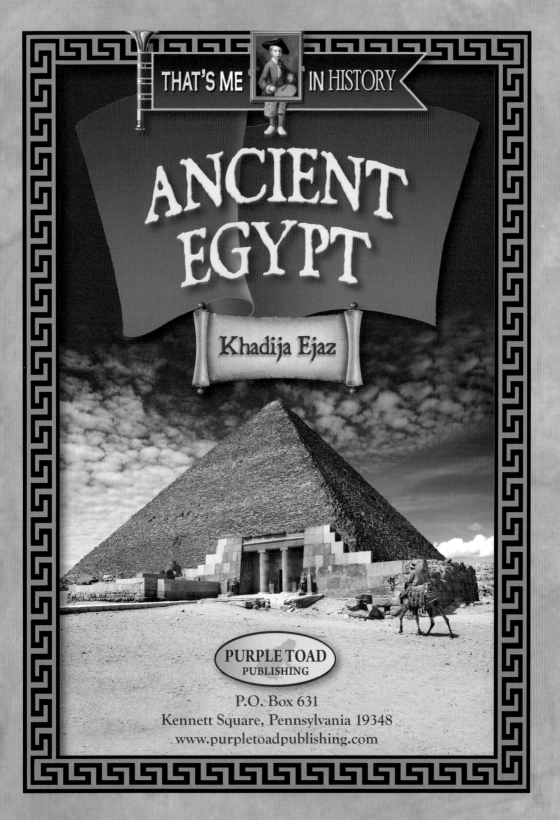

THAT'S ME IN HISTORY

ANCIENT EGYPT

Khadija Ejaz

PURPLE TOAD
PUBLISHING

P.O. Box 631
Kennett Square, Pennsylvania 19348
www.purpletoadpublishing.com

To my husband, Sonal, who thinks Pepi reminds him of his younger self.

—K.E.

ANCIENT EGYPT
MEDIEVAL ENGLAND
MING DYNASTY CHINA
RENAISSANCE ITALY
THE SPANISH EMPIRE

PUBLISHER'S NOTE: The following story has been thoroughly researched, and the documenation of such research can be found on page 46. While every possible effort has been made to ensure accuracy, the publisher will not assume liability for damages caused by inaccuracies in the data and makes no warranty on the accuracy of the information contained herein.

ABOUT THE AUTHOR: Khadija Ejaz is an internationally published and translated poet and the author of four books. She was born in Lucknow, India, raised in Muscat, Oman, and has also lived in Toronto, Canada, and New Delhi, India. Ejaz now lives in the United States, where she earned her undergraduate and graduate degrees in information technology. She has also worked in broadcast journalism at NDTV (New Delhi Television) and dabbles in filmmaking and photography. To learn more about Ejaz, visit her web site at http://khadijaejaz.netfirms.com.

Printing   1   2   3   4   5   6   7   8   9

Library of Congress
Ejaz, Khadija
  Ancient Egypt / Khadija Ejaz
    p. cm.—(That's me in history)
Includes bibliographic references and index.
ISBN: 978-1-62469-044-0 (library bound)
1. Egypt—Civilization—To 332 B.C.—Juvenile literature.
2. Egypt—History—To 332 B.C.—Juvenile literature.   I. Title.
 DT61 2013
 932.01—dc23
                                        2013936509

eBook ISBN: 9781624690457

Printed by Lake Book Manufacturing, Chicago, IL

CONTENTS

INTRODUCTION:
Pepi's Prayer

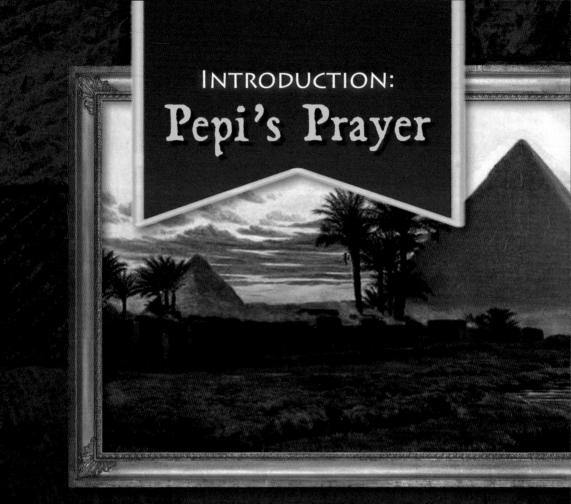

O great lord Thoth of the crescent beak:

It is I, Pepi.

Help me, dear lord. I do not want to go to scribal school. I have heard that the teachers are very strict and that the students work all day and don't get time to play. The teachers even beat the students if they don't do well.[1] How will I spend five years in a place like that?

Dear lord Thoth, I don't want to leave my friends, my family, or my cat. I do not want to be with strangers at a scary new school. And what if I am a bad student and my family is ashamed of me? Then everyone will say, "Look, there goes Pepi, the so-called son of a great scribe!"

I told Father that I do not want to go to school, and he said that he is going to take me to meet some scribes so that I will feel better about it. We are going to start meeting them tomorrow, so please help me be brave.

Sunset at the pyramids of Giza near Mennefer (modern Memphis) in Lower Egypt.

Thank you for listening to me, dear lord. I know you must be very busy inspiring all the scribes and doctors who pray to you for knowledge. Nowadays I am not sure if I should pray to you or to the Aten, so I pray to you first because I have known you longer and then I repeat the same prayer to the Aten. You must have noticed, so please don't get angry with me if I make a mistake.

I am almost done. Please bless my family, my cat, and my friends. Please bless the baby inside my mother's stomach. Please bless everyone in my city, in my land, and in every land in the world. Please remind the other gods of my name and tell them that I remember them, too.

Good night, dear lord. May the great sun god Ra make safe passage tonight through the dark underworld of Duat and be reborn again through mother Nut of the sky tomorrow morning and every morning after that.

CHAPTER 1
The Farmer's Son

I am alive. I am strong. I have awakened. My body will not be destroyed in this eternal land.[1]

Oh, hello, I remember you from last night. You were there when I was praying. I am on my way to meet my friend, Nebka. He is the son of a farmer who lives and works on my father's land. I am Pepi. Come with me, and I will show you around.

We are just outside Waset, a city in Upper Kemet in the south. If you travel north, you will enter Lower Kemet where our rocky valley ends and spreads out into a fertile delta. That is where *itroo*, the river Nile, empties out into *wadj-wer*, the great green sea. We all live along the sacred river. Today, we are in year five of the reign of Akhenaten, second month of *peret*, day eighteen.

My father is Merneptah, and he is a famous *sesh* in Waset. He is a scribe, a man who knows how to read and write. My mother is Menwi, and I have an elder sister called Neferu. My

The Karnak Temple Complex near Waset. The city was already the spiritual hub of Egypt by the time the pharaoh Akhenaten came to power in 1352 BCE. His reign lasted until 1336 BCE.

younger brother is called Qa'a. Neferu is fourteen years old and Qa'a is only five. I am ten. Neferu is engaged to be married, but she has to wait because her fiancé is in the pharaoh's army and away on a mission in Nubia on Egypt's southern borders. My mother is going to have a baby soon—we are all excited about that! I also have a cat. Her name is Nut, and she is as black as the night sky that the goddess Nut wears as her skin.

I am going to start school soon. My father is going to help me prepare by introducing me to some scribes. He was busy this morning— he is an important man—so I thought that I'd visit Nebka. I don't know how old he is, and he doesn't know, either, but we are both the same height, so I think that maybe he is ten years old as I am.

Look, you can see the Nile from here. See how it shimmers in the sunlight? I like to lie in the shade under the swaying palm trees and watch the boats go by. There is always someone traveling on the water—traders, tourists, soldiers, fishermen, priests. Nebka and I like to

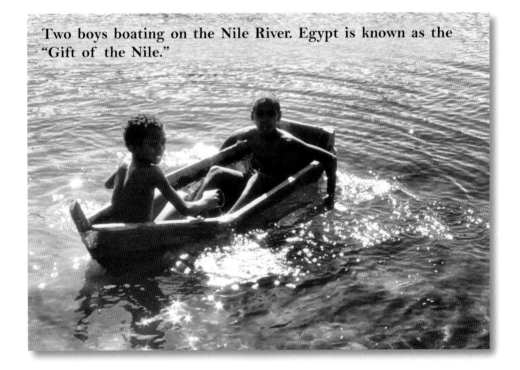

Two boys boating on the Nile River. Egypt is known as the "Gift of the Nile."

A *nekhau,* or fish amulet, from ancient Egypt. These were believed to protect from drowning by giving the wearer the swimming power of a fish. Children often wore these amulets in their hair.

come here at night to swim in the shallow parts of the river. We don't go too far; there are a lot of crocodiles and hippopotamuses in the Nile that make it a dangerous place. We know the safe parts, though, so we swim there after a quick prayer of protection to the crocodile goddess Sobek. We also carry fish amulets that keep us from drowning. Father likes to bring my family here to hunt hippopotamuses, ducks, and fish. He has also hunted lions, bulls, antelopes, and hares in the desert and has promised to take me with him when I am older.

I feel sad that I won't be able to play with Nebka once I start going to school. We have known each other since we were very little. He is my best friend. Some people don't like that I am friends with the son of a farmer. They say that I ought to mingle with those of my class, but I won't abandon Nebka.

Here we are at Nebka's house. It is made of mud bricks like all the houses in Kemet. Nebka's house has three small rooms and a staircase

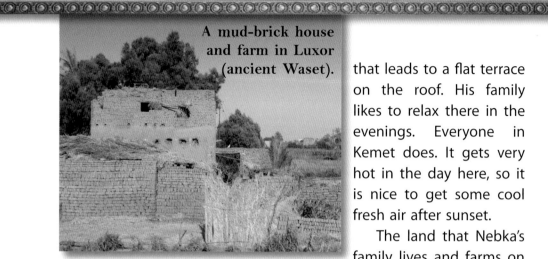

A mud-brick house and farm in Luxor (ancient Waset).

that leads to a flat terrace on the roof. His family likes to relax there in the evenings. Everyone in Kemet does. It gets very hot in the day here, so it is nice to get some cool fresh air after sunset.

The land that Nebka's family lives and farms on is owned by my father, and they pay him rent and taxes by giving him part of their harvest. We also have other farmers living and working on our land. I have heard that they are grateful for my father's kindness. Some farmers are taxed so much by their landowners that they run away; they are punished if they are caught.[2]

I am glad that Nebka and his family don't have to live that way. Life is difficult for those who do physical labor. Many people only live into their mid-thirties.[3]

Every year when the Nile floods, the farmers go to work as laborers. The flood has receded now, and the farmers are back tilling their soil and planting their crops. The main crops that are grown in Kemet are barley, wheat, and flax, but we also grow beans, dates, grapes, and figs and raise geese, pigs, cattle, and bees.

Let us enter Nebka's house. Can you see the little mud shrine in the corner? It is for Khnum, the ram-headed god of the Nile. He controls the silt that the river leaves behind after the flood. Every family in Kemet prays to certain patron gods for good fortune in their daily lives. Mine prays to Thoth, who brought writing and medicine to our people. We pray to him because we are a family of scribes. Scribes do a lot of important things, like writing government letters, collecting taxes, transcribing court cases, and overseeing royal construction projects.

There are very few scribes in Kemet, so being one is prestigious. Father says so.

Nebka's family has just had a simple breakfast of bread, cucumbers, and beer, and he is setting out with his father and brothers to work in the fields. Nebka had seven brothers and five sisters, but three boys and two girls died when they were very young. His sisters stay at home and help their mother with the cooking, cleaning, and weaving. In Kemet, the women make our clothes by weaving flax into linen. The men wear short kilts, and the women wear long, pleated, sleeveless tunics with one or two shoulder straps that may or may not cover their breasts.

Some ancient Egyptians believed that the god Khnum created human beings out of clay on a potter's wheel. Others thought that another god, Ptah, created the universe by speaking the names of everything in it.

Nebka says that he can stay behind and play with me for a short time. We like to race, wrestle, and play with his clay animal toys. His sisters play with wooden dolls as my sister does. I sometimes bring my toys to share with Nebka. My toy weapons and leather balls are his favorites.

It was a few days ago that I told Nebka about Father sending me to school. He was very happy for me. He said that learning to read and write is a gift from Thoth.

Nebka will never receive that gift. He is a farmer's son, and we in Kemet learn our trade from our fathers. Only a few are ever blessed with Thoth's gift.

LIVING BY THE NILE

Egypt has had many names. The word "Egypt" comes from "Aigyptos," the name the Greeks gave to Hikaptah, a temple complex in Mennefer (modern Memphis). The ancient Egyptians called their land Ta-Mery ("beloved land") and Kemet ("black land"). Black was the color of life. It was the color of *iqdon,* the fertile silt that the Nile deposited along its banks every year during the summertime flood. The forbidding desert around Egypt was called Daghret, the "red land." At one time, Waset (ancient Thebes or modern Luxor) was Egypt's capital.

The Nile taught the ancient Egyptians about creation, death, and rebirth. They believed that the gods and the world had been created from a cosmic river called Nun[4] and that heaven was a fertile land surrounded by water.[5] The Nile also functioned as the main highway of Egypt and connected the people to the Mediterranean Sea in the north and to Central Africa in the south.

The ancient Egyptian calendar was based on the annual flooding of the Nile. The year was divided into three seasons: *akhet* (June–September), the period of the flood; *peret* (October–January), the sowing season; and *shemu* (February–May), the time of the harvest. The calendar was twelve months long. Each month had thirty days, which were divided into three ten-day weeks. Five days were added to the end of the year and named after the gods. The day was divided into twelve hours of day and twelve hours of night, but the hours were not further divided into minutes or seconds.

The ancient Egyptians also tracked time with water clocks, sundials, and by the reigns of the pharaohs.

Elephants and hippopotamuses along the Nile River. Some historical records suggest that the first pharaoh, Menes (or Narmer), was killed by a hippo.

CHAPTER 2
The House of Merneptah

Look, there is no profession without a boss,
except for the scribe—he is the boss.[1]

Aren't you glad that we are back at my home?
Even though it is wintertime, the sun is hot.
Let me show you my home, and then we will
join my family for lunch. Oh look! It's Nut, my
cat! Come here, my dear *miu,* and meet my
new friend.

As you can see, my house is much bigger
than Nebka's. My father is a rich man; he owns
this villa just outside of Waset. Within the walls
of our estate are our house and the servants'
quarters. All the land we own lies outside of
the walls. Our house is two stories high, has
eleven rooms, a basement, and a shaded
garden. Guests are received and entertained
on the lower floor, and the top floor is where
our family sleeps. Qa'a, Neferu, and I like the
garden. We have a small pond there that is

An Egyptian boy uses a shaduf to water his home's garden.

stocked with lotus plants and fish. Nut sometimes falls in because she wants to catch the fish!

Our kitchen is in the back, away from the other rooms, so the house won't smell of food. I wouldn't mind if it did—our cooks are the best, and their food always smells good.

Let me know if you need to go to the bathroom. Most people relieve themselves outdoors, but in my house we use a wooden stool that has a hole in the middle and a bowl underneath. The bowl is emptied in the streets or into a pit in the ground.

If you want to freshen up, one of the servants will help you. You can bathe in a shallow stone tub in which you can stand and lather up with soap made of ash, scented oils, and alkaline salts. You can even use some of our creams and lotions.

My mother has many servants to help her. She and my sister even have maids to help them get dressed. Our servants are very important to us; we wouldn't be able to run our household without them. We even need them after we die. Most people have *shabti* dolls placed in their tombs so that they can help the deceased in the afterlife. I have heard that some pharaohs are buried with hundreds of them![2]

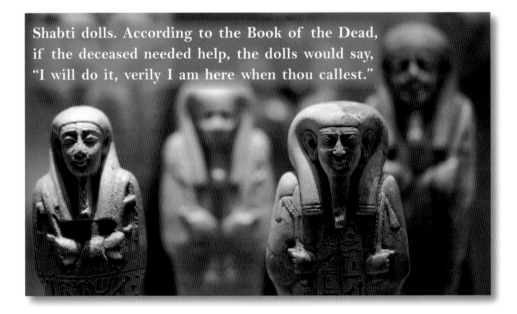

Shabti dolls. According to the Book of the Dead, if the deceased needed help, the dolls would say, "I will do it, verily I am here when thou callest."

A Mehen game board

My house has a flat roof like the one at Nebka's, and we often host banquets there. We are going to have one in a few days, and you are invited. We also like to relax there in the evenings and play board games like Senet, Mehen (which is played on a board shaped like a snake), and "hounds and jackals."

Most of the houses here are painted white with lime plaster so that they stay cool in the hot sun. Mother likes to make things pretty so she had artists paint murals on our walls. All the rooms have small windows high on the walls. We keep them covered with reed curtains so that the rooms stay cool. We light the house after sunset with oil lamps, but we don't keep them burning for long. We like to sleep once it gets dark so that we can wake up with the sunrise.

We have shrines in our house, too. You already know that my family worships Thoth, but we also worship Bes and Hathor, because they protect children. My mother is going to have a baby soon, so she prays to lord Bes and mother Hathor for health and protection. She also carries their amulets with her.

It is time for lunch. Let us go to the dining room. One of the servants will come get Nut; she has to have her meal, too! Some of our people worship a cat goddess called Bastet. She is the daughter of Ra and patron of a city called Per-Bastet in the delta. When Nut dies, we will embalm her body and bury her in a cat cemetery nearby. My sister also has a pet—a dove she loves very much that was a present from her fiancé.

Since it is lunchtime, my family is sitting on reed mats around a low table. Our servants will bring the food in a few minutes. Come, let us join them.

An Egyptian boy wearing his hair as the S-shaped side-lock of youth.

Are you comfortable? It can get quite hot in Kemet—it almost never rains—which is why we all wear white linen garments and reed sandals. My family dresses like Nebka's family does, except that our linen is finer. My brother is too young to wear clothes; the children in our land only start wearing clothes when they are around six years old.

Qa'a and I shave our heads except for one long lock of hair on one side. All boys wear it as a mark of youth, and they shave it all off when they turn twelve. Young girls wear pigtails, and adults wear their hair very short. Many men shave their heads. Women style their hair in different ways. They wear extensions and elaborate wigs that are made of human hair, wool, or vegetable fibers, and are attached to the scalp using beeswax. You can see why my mother and sister need a maid just for that!

Women took great care of their appearance. They wore different kinds of wigs and used kohl to decorate their eyes.

I wonder what the cooks have made for us today. We eat with our hands and enjoy all sorts of meat, particularly fish and beef, but we don't eat lamb for religious reasons.[3] The meat is served with vegetables like spinach, lentils, and onions. We love bread—we have fifteen different words for it![4] We drink sweet, thick beer with our food and often enjoy fresh melons or figs for dessert.

Father plans to take me to meet some scribes this afternoon. He is a senior scribe and oversees junior scribes and artisans. I am nervous, so I am glad you will be there with me.

THE SOCIAL PYRAMID

Ancient Egyptian society was shaped like a pyramid. At the top was the pharaoh, the living god. The word "pharaoh" comes from *per-aa,* which means "royal house," but over time came to refer to the *nesoo* (ruler) himself.

Below the pharaoh came the royal family, and below them were priests and royal advisors, and then scribes. They were followed by craftsmen, and then farmers. Servants and slaves were found at the bottom of society.

The pharaoh was the head of the government and the priest of every temple, but he designated those roles to a *tjaty* (vizier) and to the priesthood. Under the vizier, the land was divided into forty-two regions called *nomes,* which were governed by nomarchs.[5] Each nome had its own capital city and patron gods.

Trades were passed down from father to son, and only one in a hundred Egyptians knew how to read or write. The only schools were the ones that provided scribal training to the sons of the wealthy to prepare them to enter the bureaucracy. Some rich families tutored their children at home.

Egyptian women enjoyed more freedom than Greek and Roman women. Common women could own property, even after marriage. They did not go to school, but they were sometimes trained at home and could work outdoors and run businesses.

Egyptian society encouraged marriage, and women were respected as wives and mothers. By law, a man could marry as many women as he wished, but most common men had only one wife. The pharaoh had many, but named one as his chief wife. The lives of royal women, though, were very restricted. Most were married to their fathers, grandfathers, brothers, and sons to protect property and the royal bloodline. Some were even married off to the gods as priestesses.[6]

Pharaoh Akhenaten, of the eighteenth dynasty, struggled with the powerful priests of Waset.

The pharaoh wore the tall white crown (hedjet) of Upper Egypt, the shorter red crown (deshret) of Lower Egypt, or a double crown (pschent) if he governed both lands. He also wore a blue helmetlike crown (khepresh), a striped cloth headdress (nemes), or a single-colored headdress (khat). Egyptian men were clean-shaven, but the pharaoh always wore a ceremonial beard.

CHAPTER 3
Doorway to the Afterlife

*As for writing, it is profitable to him
who knows it . . .
Pleasanter than bread and beer . . .
It is more precious than a heritage in Egypt.
Than a tomb in the West.*[1]

Here we are on the western bank of the Nile. Did you enjoy our boat ride across the river? Most people travel in boats made of papyrus reeds that have been tightly sewn together. These boats are very sturdy; our people are expert shipbuilders. My family's boat is nicer—it is made of wooden planks from the cedar tree, which grows in a foreign land called Phoenicia. We even have people to row for us.

I don't usually get to visit this side of the river. Most people in Kemet live on the eastern bank. That is where we build all our cities because east is where the sun rises and where life begins. The west is where the sun sets and

An example of a cedar boat powered by oars that would have been seen on the Nile.

life ends, and that is why we build tombs on this side of the river. That is part of the reason we are here today.

My father is supervising the building of his tomb where he will be buried after he dies. He wants me to meet Hesy-Ra, one of his junior scribes. Father likes him because he learns quickly and has good character.

Look, here comes Hesy-Ra with his scribal palette and brush. He is quite young, maybe a few years older than Neferu. He, too, is from a scribal family. He did so well at scribal school that he was recommended to my father as an apprentice. What a friendly smile Hesy-Ra has, and such nice teeth! You will not see too many people in Kemet with good teeth because the sand that gets into our bread grinds our teeth down over time.[2] Father is going to inspect the site while I chat with Hesy-Ra and learn more about what it's like to be a junior scribe.

Hesy-Ra says he works on a team with other junior scribes and is coming up with designs and writing that will adorn the walls of Father's tomb. The pictures will show my father, our family, and the gods. The writing will be about Father's life and include spells that will help him find his way past the snakes and demons of the underworld into the afterlife.[3]

Look at the walls. Do you see the grids that have been drawn on them? Hesy-Ra says that the junior scribes use the grids to scale up their designs from their papyrus drawings.[4] One small grid on their papyrus equals one big grid on the wall.

They draw their designs on the wall with red ink, and Father makes corrections with black ink. The pens are made from reeds and the different inks are made from things like charcoal, soot, crushed minerals, and red earth. Once Father has approved the designs, the artisans will start bringing them to life by carving reliefs out of them and painting them with bright colors.

It must be such an honor to know the divine gift of writing. Each symbol is a picture of an object that represents a sound or an idea, and I have heard that at scribal school they teach you how to write more

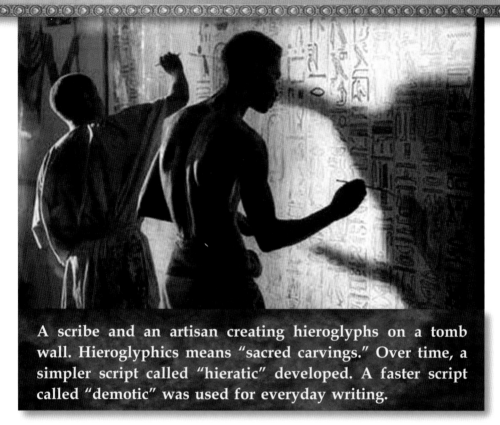

A scribe and an artisan creating hieroglyphs on a tomb wall. Hieroglyphics means "sacred carvings." Over time, a simpler script called "hieratic" developed. A faster script called "demotic" was used for everyday writing.

than seven hundred of them. Students are also taught mathematics and the languages of the people of Canaan, Phoenicia, and Babylon. They practice their symbols on pieces of pottery and stone, but real scribes write on sheets made from the papyrus reed that grows along the Nile.

Hesy-Ra is proud of the work that has been happening here. He tells me that Father designed this tomb to have a courtyard and a chapel cut into the rocks. Father also has a statue of himself that faces east into the rising sun, so that after he dies, he will be reborn like Ra every morning. There is also an underground burial chamber from where he shall start his journey into the Field of Reeds in the next life. The walls bear his name—to speak the name of the dead is to make them live again.

People who can afford it start building their tombs while they are alive. Those who can't afford a tomb are buried in graves, but everyone is buried with food and other belongings that will be of use to them in the next life. The pharaoh and the nobility are buried with great treasures.

The old pharaohs who used to rule from Mennefer in the delta region built their tombs as pyramids. But Waset is in a valley, and we don't have the flat land to build these *mers,* so we cut tombs deep into the mountains instead. That way maybe grave robbers won't be able to plunder the tombs the way they did with the pyramids. Hesy-Ra says many tomb robbers are laborers who helped build the tombs, and that some government officials and priests allowed them steal and then demanded a share of the treasure. How horrible!

Father's tomb is not the only one here. This is a necropolis; a lot of pharaohs and their families are buried here in areas we call "The Great Place" and "The Place of Beauties." In the old days, it was only the

"The Great Place" is now called "The Valley of the Kings." "The Place of Beauties," which today is known as "The Valley of the Queens," also used to be called "The Place of the Children of the Pharaoh" in ancient times.

The tomb of the pharaoh Tutankhamun in the "Valley of the Kings" in Egypt. Tutankhamun was Akhenaten's successor.

royalty whose bodies were preserved by Anubis and buried in tombs, but nowadays everyone does it: kings, queens, and their families; noblemen; scribes; and even common people. Anubis is the god of embalming, and he has the head of a jackal. His body is black because that is the color of life, and he helps us live in the afterlife.

It takes many years to build a tomb, and it takes even more people. There are villages nearby, on this bank of the river, which house the workers and their families. People like the pharaohs also build mortuary temples outside of their tombs where priests worship them all year long.

To the south of where we stand is the palace of Amenhotep. He was the father of our current pharaoh, Akhenaten. I asked Father if we could visit it, but he said that Akhenaten doesn't live there anymore. He said that the pharaoh has built a palace in a new city north of here, which he named Akhetaten. Akhetaten is supposed to be the new capital of Kemet. But what about Waset? Does that mean Waset is not the most important city in Kemet anymore?

BEYOND THE FINAL JOURNEY

Life and death were serious business to the ancient Egyptians. They loved life and wanted it to continue after death, which is why they preserved the bodies of the dead as mummies. They believed in an afterlife where the dead lived in a perfect world, an everlasting field of reeds. They believed a person was made up of their physical body, their *ba* (personality), their *ka* (spiritual twin), their *akh* (made up of the *ba* and *ka*), their shadow, and their name, all of which were needed to make passage into the next life.[5] They feared criminal punishment that involved death by fire because it would destroy the body and erase the person's spiritual existence.[6]

Upon dying, which was called "crossing to the other bank," the dead person would be led by the god Anubis into the underworld, called Duat, and into the Hall of Two Truths. Spells that were inscribed on the walls of the tomb (called Pyramid Texts) and inside the coffin (called Coffin Texts) were meant to help the soul bypass any dangers along the way. These spells were later combined into the Book of the Dead, which was often placed between the legs of the mummy as it was being wrapped in linen.

In the Hall of Two Truths, the deceased's heart was measured against the feather of Ma'at (the goddess of justice) on the Scales of Justice by the ibis-headed god Thoth. The deceased would be allowed to move into the afterlife if his or her heart was judged to be pure. If his or her deeds did not measure up, however, the person would be consumed by a fearsome demon called Ammut. Ammut was also called the Devourer of the Dead and the Eater of Hearts.

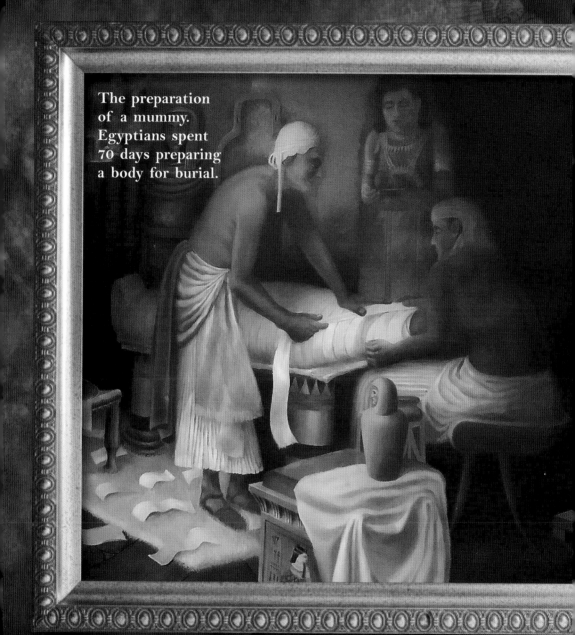

The preparation of a mummy. Egyptians spent 70 days preparing a body for burial.

CHAPTER 4

City of Amun

Splendid you rise in heaven's lightland,
O living Aten, creator of life![1]

Behold Ipet-Isut, the "most select of places," the great temple of Amun. Amun is the hidden god, the god of the breath of life, and we worship him, his wife, Mut, and their son, Khonsu, here in Waset. In Mennefer, they worship another divine family, that of Ptah, Sekhmet, and Nefertum.

We are here to meet the priest Rahotep, who is a friend of my father's. I am excited about meeting him after spending time with Hesy-Ra yesterday. Priests are scribes too, and they are the ones who train young scribes like Hesy-Ra. Maybe Rahotep will end up becoming my teacher. I hope he will be nice to me!

This temple is part of a large complex that is dedicated to Amun and his family. It includes schools, libraries, storerooms, and living quarters for the priests and workmen. There are many levels of priests, and all of them work together to help run the temple economy. The

Pillars of the Great
Hypostyle Hall from the
Precinct of Amun-Re in
Karnak. The Hypostyle
Hall was built by the
pharaoh Seti I.

A sphinx from the avenue that connects Karnak and "Amun's Southern Harem," the Luxor Temple. These sphinxes were first built by the eighteenth-dynasty pharaoh Amenhotep III. By the thirtieth dynasty, they numbered to over a thousand.

pharaohs started building this complex many years ago, and each pharaoh adds on to it. The complex is built along the river's eastern bank and can be reached through a canal that leads up to the temple's harbor. An avenue of sphinxes connects this complex to another fabulous temple called Amun's Southern Harem.

I know I am still young, but this place makes me feel even smaller. Look at the sheer size of the monuments here—the soaring gold-tipped obelisks that glint in the sun, the towers and flags that stretch into the sky, the colossal statues that silently watch over the world. It is almost like a fortress. Our temples are made of stone, unlike our houses and even the royal palaces, which are made of mud bricks. Do you see the brightly colored sculptures and the writing all over the outside wall? These were also designed by scribes. Imagine the honor!

Temples are not meant for the public. They are the houses of the gods where priests tend to their needs so that they will continue to protect us. Most temples are built within high walls with obelisks and a grand pylon entrance on the outside. Come, let us go inside.

This large courtyard is the farthest we will be allowed to go; only the priests and the pharaoh are allowed to go inside. Beyond this courtyard is a huge covered hall with lots of tall pillars—the hypostyle hall—and after that lies a smaller hall called the Hall of Offerings. In the heart of the temple is the sanctuary where a gold statue of the patron god is housed in a shrine.

We call the priests *hem netjer,* which means "servant of god." Twice a day the priests bathe the statue of the god and offer it food and perfume, and each time they have to purify themselves in the sacred temple lakes for the ritual. They also have to shave all the hair on their bodies, even their eyebrows!

Here comes Rahotep. Did I tell you that he is actually a *soonoo* (doctor) and only works as a priest for three months out of the year?[2] Many priests do that, and a number of them specialize in the healing arts. They are able to help people with their teeth, digestion, breathing, eyes, fertility, and bones. They use strange medicines and secret spells for their cures.

Doctors are trained at the House of Life, which is a school that is attached to a temple. These schools store a lot of secret knowledge. Rahotep says that at these schools, the students can learn to talk to animals![3]

Rahotep is upset. He says that our pharaoh, Akhenaten, has decreed the new god Aten to be the only god. All the temples in Kemet are being shut down, and the names and images of all the gods are being struck off of the public buildings. Even the name of Amun from his father's name is being removed. Rahotep says that Akhenaten will anger the gods and bring ruin to all of us, but we are forced to obey his edict. Still, how can only one god watch over all of Kemet?

I wonder what will happen to our festivals; most of them honor the gods. During the Nile's annual flood, Osiris is remembered at the Sokar and Nehebkau festivals. We celebrate Min, the god of fertility, during the harvest. The biggest festivals in Waset are dedicated to Amun and his family. During the Opet Festival, people gather to watch as Amun's priests carry his statue down the river to his Southern Harem. The statues of his family are taken across the Nile to the necropolis in the west during the Valley Feast.

Many people approach the gods during these processions to ask for guidance. People ask for help from the gods in other ways, too. My mother visits the temple's hearing wall where she can speak her troubles into an ear-shaped hole. Amun speaks back to her from the other side, but some people say that it is actually the priests who do the talking.[4] She also asks the priests about the meaning of her dreams.

Will we still be allowed to mark the jubilee of the pharaoh at the Sed Festival? That happens in the thirtieth year of the pharaoh's reign, and Akhenaten has not been on the throne long. I do not know what will happen when that time comes.

Rahotep encourages my going to school. He says that I might grow up to become a powerful priest or a famous doctor. Mother has been seeing doctors regularly because she is pregnant. They once asked her to urinate on seeds of barley and emmer wheat—the emmer wheat sprouted first, so we learned that I will soon have another sister![5]

Let us visit the market before we return to my home. I thought we'd walk because it is nearby, so make sure your sandals are strapped on tight! I already sent home the palanquin that we came here on. You won't see too many people riding on palanquins in Kemet; it is a luxury to ride on an expensive covered chair that is carried by strong bearers. Most people walk, ride the *a-aa* (donkey), or sail on the Nile.

Like most of Kemet's cities, Waset is surrounded by thick, high walls. The temple forms the center, and the city spreads out around it. The nice neighborhoods are where the nobility, government officials, army officers, and wealthy merchants live. The rest of the people like the artisans, workers, and peasants occupy the other parts. The marketplace is where everyone comes together.

And here we are! Give yourself a minute to take in the sights of this busy place. Can you smell the honey cakes from the baker's stall? The market is where buyers and sellers exchange goods. They haggle and

A marketplace in ancient Egypt. Markets were usually set up near the Nile. For most of Egypt's history, the people did not use currency. They followed a barter system where they exchanged items according to their perceived value.

negotiate the value of the exchange in copper weights called *deben.* One *deben* is made up of ten *kite,* and ten *deben* make up one *sep.* You ought to see my mother bargain with the sellers!

There is always something or someone interesting here. You can find stonemasons selling alabaster cosmetic jars, weavers selling baskets, and glassmakers and jewelry makers selling beautiful *wesekh* collar necklaces. You might even find a tattoo artist or a merchant selling slaves and exotic animals like ostriches and apes.

Some of the stalls sell everyday items like vegetables, meat, linen, and papyrus, but others carry items that have been brought from distant towns in Kemet or even from faraway lands. Some of our merchants have become rich by importing items like copper, incense, ebony, ivory, spices, and colorful stones and gems.

Can you spot the foreign merchants? They're the ones wearing colorful clothes. I love to hear them call out to customers in their exotic accents. One stroll through the marketplace, and I feel like I have traveled the world!

A ROYAL HERESY

The ancient Egyptians worshiped hundreds of gods. One myth speaks of the god Atum who rose on a mound in the primeval waters and created Shu (god of the air) and his sister-wife, Tefnut (goddess of moisture). They gave birth to Geb (god of the earth) and his sister-wife, Nut (goddess of the sky), who in turn gave birth to Osiris, Isis, Seth, and Nephthys, from whom a number of other gods like Horus and Anubis were born. The pharaoh was considered to be the human embodiment of Horus.

There were two kinds of gods in ancient Egypt—the state gods of a city and temple, and the everyday household gods. Every home had its own patron god, and cult cities dedicated to particular deities thrived all across Egypt. But by the eighteenth dynasty, the pharaoh Akhenaten decided to overthrow them all with one of the earliest monotheistic movements.

Akhenaten was born as Amenhotep IV, son of the pharaoh Amenhotep III. During his reign (1352 BCE–1336 BCE) he banished worship of all the traditional Egyptian gods in favor of the Aten, the solar disc, of which he made himself a prophet. Akhenaten's name means "Servant of the Aten," and some historians believe that his wife Nefertiti was renamed Neferneferuaten, which means "Beautiful is the Beauty of the Aten." She was not his only wife, but there is evidence that she was his favorite.

The new religion was not popular, and it threatened the powerful priesthood of Thebes, which was the capital of Egypt at the time. Akhenaten built a new capital called Akhetaten, which means "Horizon of Aten." Today, this archaeological site is called el-Amarna. Some

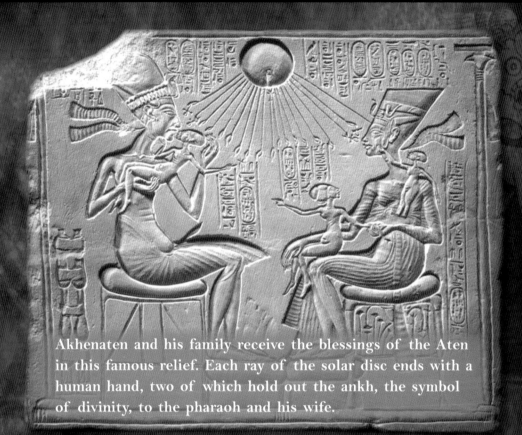

Akhenaten and his family receive the blessings of the Aten in this famous relief. Each ray of the solar disc ends with a human hand, two of which hold out the ankh, the symbol of divinity, to the pharaoh and his wife.

historians believe that a plague killed many people there, including Akhenaten and most of his family.[6] After Akhenaten's death, his successor Tutankhamun brought back worship of the traditional gods of Egypt. Originally named Tutankhaten ("Living Image of Aten"), he changed his name to Tutankhamun ("Living Image of Amun") to show his rejection of his father's cult. Akhenaten was vilified as a heretic by all the pharaohs that followed him, and the priesthood kept a close eye on the pharaoh from then on.

CHAPTER 5
The Warrior at the Banquet

With a beaming face celebrate the joyful day and rest not therein. For no one can take away his goods with him. Yea no one returns again, who has gone hence.[1]

This is a special banquet. My sister Neferu's fiancé, Userkaf, is back. They hadn't seen each other for a year, and she waited for him to return so that they can marry. Most girls in Kemet get married when they enter womanhood around the age of twelve, but Neferu chose to wait for Userkaf. He is twenty years old and an officer in the pharaoh's permanent army. Can you see him sitting next to my father at the banquet table? Userkaf's father, who is a friend of Father's, is a decorated general—he was awarded the Golden Fly necklace by the pharaoh for "stinging" the enemy in a battle with the Libyans.

An Egyptian wedding banquet

Userkaf was away in Nubia leading a military expedition, but he is back now and will be supervising royal construction projects for a while. His recent mission won him a gift of land from the pharaoh. I have heard that he has a good future in the army. The pharaohs are traditionally chosen from within the royal family, but I have heard that in our history some officers have become viziers and even pharaohs. I am happy for my sister, she will have a good life.

Father had asked me to talk to Userkaf because the army has scribes, too. Earlier today, Userkaf told me about the life of a soldier. Most positions are passed down from father to son, but many young men without any connections to the army can sign up for service. Slaves can win their freedom by enlisting in the army, and the pharaoh also hires foreign mercenaries to fight for him.

Userkaf started training for army life when he was only five years old. He had to learn how to wrestle, throw knives, drive a chariot pulled by high-spirited horses, and use a *khepesh,* which is a curved sword. It is not a glamorous life, he told me, because soldiers have to go on long marches and carry their belongings, weapons, and armor with them. They suffer terrible injuries during battle. Userkaf encouraged me to become a scribe because that way I could still work in the army but be safe and comfortable.

Military scribes do many things. They go with the army onto the battlefield, send messages, and record events (sometimes in the form

Egyptian chariots are thought to have been adopted from Asiatic people called "the Hyksos" around 1600 BCE.

of poetry), including the amount of spoils and the number of prisoners taken. Userkaf says that scribes also record the number of fallen soldiers by counting amputated body parts on the battlefield.[2]

Userkaf told me a secret! He asked a scribe in his division to write a love poem for Neferu. He is reciting the poem now. I will translate for you:

She looks like the rising morning star,
At the start of a happy year,
Shining bright, fair of skin,
Lovely the look of her eyes,
Sweet the speech of her lips . . .
With graceful step she treads the ground,
Captures my heart by her movements,
She causes all men's necks,
To turn about to see her;
Joy has he whom she embraces,
He is like the first of men![3]

Look at my sister and my mother sitting next to each other at the table—they are holding hands and smiling at Userkaf. How their dark eyes shine! My mother really likes him, and she is very excited about the wedding next month. She has even started working on the menu for the wedding banquet. It is going to be much bigger than this one. That is how weddings are performed here—unions are announced and celebrated at banquets where the families get together with their friends to enjoy food, music, poetry, and dancing. Divorce is easy, too. All you have to do is announce it in public.

This is my favorite time of the year for terrace-top banquets. Have you tried all the dishes our cooks have made? Tonight they have served us barbequed gazelle and roasted heron with garlic, dates, beans, and leeks. Mother insisted on including lotus roots and cheese because it is a special occasion. I can't wait for dessert—fruits, pastries, and cakes sweetened with honey and shaped like crocodiles. And wine!

Do you like what the musicians are playing for us? I always like to watch the dancing girls. Some of them are pretty, and many of them sing very well. When the music and the songs are good, the guests like to clap along. Tonight the musicians are playing the harp, flutes, drums, tambourines, cymbals, and lutes.

My father knows a lot of important people, and many of them are here tonight with their families. Nebka could not be invited because he is from a poor family, and I am sad about that. But everyone seems to be enjoying themselves. Our servants helped all the female guests attach cones of scented animal fat to their wigs. When the fat melts, the oil drips down people's bodies and releases a perfume. They have also been distributing lotus flowers and flower garlands to everyone.

The guests have shown up tonight in makeup, jewelry, nice clothes, and fancy wigs. The women have colored their toenails, hands, and feet with henna and are dressed in fashionable fringed tunics, some of them sheer. Some of the men are wearing cloaks in addition to their kilts. Both the men and the women are wearing jewelry—rings, bracelets, earrings, anklets, necklaces—made of gold, the skin of the gods, and silver, the bones of the gods, and studded with colorful stones.[4] They have also decorated their eyes with black or green kohl. It reminds me of the *Wadjet,* the Eye of Horus, which can only be a good thing.

Look, there is Rahotep, the priest we met at the temple of Amun. He is married and has come with his wife and children. Hesy-Ra, the scribe, is here, too. He seems to be sharing a joke with Userkaf, whose parents and six younger sisters are also here. My sister likes to tease Qa'a and me and say that she will pick wives for us from Userkaf's sisters! I am glad that I won't have to worry about getting married for a few years if I go to scribal school. That alone is a good reason to go!

I shall tell father tonight that I want to attend scribal school.

Thank you, lord Thoth, for seeing me through this. And thank you, too, my new friend. *Imee dee-too en-ten ankh seneb oodja* (life, health, and prosperity to all of you)!

RESURRECTION

"My name is Ozymandias, king of kings—
Look on my works, ye Mighty, and despair!"[5]

These words are from "Ozymandias," an 1818 poem by the British poet Percy Bysshe Shelley. Some say that Ozymandias refers to Ramesses II. At the time, a statue of the pharaoh was on its way to Britain from where it had lain amidst ruins in Egypt.

Much of what we know today about ancient Egypt comes from what its people left behind in writing, but by 300 CE, their language had been abandoned and the meaning behind their symbols lost. Their writing remained unreadable until 1822 when Jean Francois Champollion deciphered it via the Rosetta Stone. This stone tablet was found by a French soldier in 1792 in el-Rashid (Rosetta) and bears inscriptions in Greek and two ancient Egyptian scripts—hieroglyphic and demotic. By comparing the scripts to the known Greek text, experts were able to read ancient Egyptian writing for the first time in over a thousand years.

The unlocking of the language of the ancient Egyptians led to a massive worldwide interest in ancient Egypt. Tourism spiked, Egyptian fashion and interior design became all the rage, and archaeologists (and treasure hunters) traveled to Egypt in droves. Ancient Egypt had captured the world's imagination.

Mummies in particular became the object of fascination. Tombs were excavated, and the resident mummies were shipped to Europe where they were displayed during public unwrappings. Powder made from crushed mummy remains was even incorporated into medicine as an important ingredient, and while on its way back to Cairo, the mummy of Ramesses II was taxed by the Egyptian government as imported dried fish![6]

BCE

8000–3400	Civilizations develop in Upper and Lower Egypt. The world's oldest known board game, Senet, is invented.
3100–2686	Early Dynastic Period. Egypt is unified by the first pharaoh, Menes/Narmer, who rules from his capital in Memphis. Hieroglyphic and hieratic develop. Papyrus and the 365-day calendar are first used. The earliest mummies are made.
2686–2181	Old Kingdom. The pyramids at Saqqara and Giza and the Sphinx are built.
2181–2055	First Intermediate Period. Egypt is reunited by a new capital at Thebes after a period of chaos by Mentuhotep II.
2055–1650	Middle Kingdom. Rock-cut tombs and the earliest parts of the Temple of Karnak are built. Egyptian physicians write the world's first medical textbook. By around 1674 BCE, much of Egypt is ruled from Avaris in the Nile Delta by Asiatic tribes called the Hyksos.
1650–1550	Second Intermediate Period. Ahmose unifies the country. The Hyksos are defeated by Egyptians from Thebes.
1550–1069	New Kingdom. (The age of great pharaohs like Seti I, Queen Hatshepsut, and Amenhotep III.) Ramesses II builds temples at Thebes and Abu Simbel. Royal tombs are built in the Valley of the Kings. The world's first glassmaking takes place in Egypt.
1350	Akhenaten introduces worship of the sun disc and creates a new capital at el-Amarna. His successors move the capital back to Memphis around 1336 BCE and restore the old cults at Thebes.
1300	The shaduf irrigation device is introduced to Egypt.
1198–1182	The Mediterranean Sea Peoples attack Egypt and are defeated by Ramesses III, the last great warrior king.
1160	Egyptian scholars draw the world's first known maps.
1069–715	Third Intermediate Period. Rival pharaohs rule across Egypt. The priesthood gains power. Demotic replaces hieratic.
747–332	Late Period. (The time of conquests by the Nubians, Assyrians, and Persians.)
332–30	Ptolemaic Period. Alexander the Great conquers Egypt in 332 BCE and builds a capital at Alexandria. Ptolemy I, one of his commanders, takes control in 305 BCE. Greek script is introduced, and the Rosetta Stone is carved around 196 BCE.
30	Cleopatra VII dies. Egypt becomes part of the Roman Empire.

CE

395	Egypt becomes part of the Byzantine Empire. Coptic replaces hieroglyphic and demotic as Christianity is introduced to Egypt.
641	The Arabs invade Egypt. Islam becomes the state religion and Arabic the official language. The city of Cairo is founded in 969.
1517	Egypt is conquered by the Turks.
1798	Napoleon Bonaparte invades Egypt. The discovery of the Rosetta Stone in 1799 allows the world to read ancient Egyptian again in 1822.
1859–1869	The Suez Canal is built. Formal excavations begin in Egypt.
1881	A group of royal mummies is found. The mummy of Ramesses II is unwrapped.
1922	Howard Carter discovers the tomb of Tutankhamun.
1953	Egypt becomes an independent country.
1960	The Aswan Dam is built.
2007	Archaeologists confirm that they have found the mummy of Queen Hatshepsut, which had been discovered in 1903.

Introduction: Pepi's Prayer
1. Lionel Casson, *Ancient Egypt* (New York: Time Inc., 1969), pp. 99–100.

Chapter 1. The Farmer's Son
1. Denise Dersin, *What Life Was Like on the Banks of the Nile* (New York: Time Life Inc., 2009), p. 179.
2. David Pickering, *Ancient Egypt* (London: Collins, 2007), pp. 132–134.
3. Milton Meltzer, *In the Day of the Pharaohs—A Look at Ancient Egypt* (Danbury, CT: Franklin Watts, 2001), pp. 25–26.
4. Charlotte Booth, *The Ancient Egyptians for Dummies* (Chichester, UK: John Wiley & Sons, 2007), p. 11.
5. David Pickering, *Ancient Egypt* (London: Collins, 2007), p. 11.

Chapter 2. The House of Merneptah
1. Charlotte Booth, *The Ancient Egyptians for Dummies* (Chichester, UK: John Wiley & Sons, 2007), p. 37.
2. David Pickering, *Ancient Egypt* (London: Collins, 2007), p. 131.
3. Milton Meltzer, *In the Day of the Pharaohs—A Look at Ancient Egypt* (Danbury, CT: Franklin Watts, 2001), p. 130.
4. Lionel Casson, *Ancient Egypt* (New York: Time Inc., 1969), p. 45.
5. Charlotte Booth, *The Ancient Egyptians for Dummies* (Chichester, UK: John Wiley & Sons, 2007), p. 16.
6. Ibid, pp. 44–52.

Chapter 3. Doorway to the Afterlife
1. Denise Dersin, *What Life Was Like on the Banks of the Nile* (New York: Time Life Inc., 2009), p. 61.
2. David Pickering, *Ancient Egypt* (London, UK: Collins, 2007), p. 137.
3. George Hart, *Ancient Egypt* (New York: Dorling Kindersley Limited, 2008), p. 33.
4. Milton Meltzer, *In the Day of the Pharaohs—A Look at Ancient Egypt* (Danbury, CT: Franklin Watts, 2001), p. 43.
5. Charlotte Booth, *The Ancient Egyptians for Dummies* (Chichester, UK: John Wiley & Sons, 2007), p. 190.
6. Donald P. Ryan, *Ancient Egypt on 5 Deben a Day* (London: Thames & Hudson Ltd., 2010), p. 25.

Chapter 4. City of Amun
1. Denise Dersin, *What Life Was Like on the Banks of the Nile* (New York: Time Life Inc., 2009), p. 91.
2. Philip Steele, *Passport to the Past—Ancient Egypt* (New York: The Rosen Publishing Group, 2009), pp. 32–33.
3. Donald P. Ryan, *Ancient Egypt on 5 Deben a Day* (London: Thames & Hudson Ltd., 2010), pp. 34–35.
4. Carmella Van Vleet, *Great Ancient Egypt Projects You Can Build Yourself* (White River Junction, VT: Nomad Press, 2006), pp. 87–92.
5. Charlotte Booth, *The Ancient Egyptians for Dummies* (Chichester, UK: John Wiley & Sons, 2007), p. 169.
6. Ibid, pp. 83–87.

Chapter 5. The Warrior at the Banquet
1. Denise Dersin, *What Life Was Like on the Banks of the Nile* (New York: Time Life Inc., 2009), p. 98.
2. Charlotte Booth, *The Ancient Egyptians for Dummies* (Chichester, UK: John Wiley & Sons, 2007), pp. 67–77.
3. Denise Dersin, *What Life Was Like on the Banks of the Nile* (New York: Time Life Inc., 2009), p. 88.
4. Donald P. Ryan, *Ancient Egypt on 5 Deben a Day* (London: Thames & Hudson Ltd., 2010), p. 22.
5. Percy Bysshe Shelley, "Ozymandias", http://www.poetryfoundation.org/poem/175903.
6. Lionel Casson, *Ancient Egypt* (New York: Time Inc., 1969), p. 77.

Books

Millmore, Mark. *Imagining Egypt—A Living Portrait of the Time of the Pharaohs.* New York: Eyelid Productions, Ltd., 2007.

Shaw, Ian. *Places in Time—Exploring Ancient Egypt.* New York: Oxford University Press, 2003.

Shaw, Ian. *The Oxford History of Ancient Egypt.* New York: Oxford University Press, 2000.

Wilkinson, Richard H. *The Complete Gods and Goddesses of Ancient Egypt.* London: Thames & Hudson Limited, 2003.

Woog, Adam. *Mummies.* San Diego, CA: ReferencePoint Press, Inc., 2009.

Works Consulted

Bernabeo, Paul. *Ancient Egypt and the Near East.* New York: Marshall Cavendish Corporation, 2011.

Bingham, Jane. *How People Lived in Ancient Egypt.* New York: Wayland/The Rosen Publishing Group Inc., 2009.

Booth, Charlotte. *The Ancient Egyptians for Dummies.* Chichester, UK: John Wiley & Sons, 2007.

Casson, Lionel. *Ancient Egypt.* New York: Time Inc., 1969.

Dersin, Denise. *What Life Was Like on the Banks of the Nile.* New York: Time Life Inc., 2009.

Hart, George. *Ancient Egypt.* New York: Dorling Kindersley Limited, 2008.

Hollar, Sherman. *Ancient Egypt.* New York: Encyclopædia Britannica, 2012.

Meltzer, Milton. *In the Day of the Pharaohs—A Look at Ancient Egypt.* Danbury, CT: Franklin Watts, 2001.

Pemberton, Delia. *The Atlas of Ancient Egypt.* New York: Harry N. Abrams, Inc., 2005.

Pickering, David. *Ancient Egypt.* London: Collins, 2007.

Ryan, Donald P. *Ancient Egypt on 5 Deben a Day.* London: Thames & Hudson Ltd., 2010.

Smith, Miranda. *Ancient Egypt.* New York: Kingfisher, 2010.

Sonneborn, Liz. *The Egyptians—Life in Ancient Egypt.* Minneapolis, MN: Lerner Publishing Group, Inc., 2010.

Steele, Philip. *Passport to the Past—Ancient Egypt.* New York: The Rosen Publishing Group, 2009.

Van Vleet, Carmella. *Great Ancient Egypt Projects You Can Build Yourself.* White River Junction, VT: Nomad Press, 2006.

On the Internet

Aldokkan: Ancient Egypt
    http://aldokkan.com

The Ancient Egypt Site
    http://www.ancient-egypt.org/index.html

BBC: History—Egyptians
    http://www.bbc.co.uk/history/ancient/egyptians/

The British Museum: Ancient Egypt
    http://www.ancientegypt.co.uk/

The Children's University of Manchester: Ancient Egypt
    http://www.childrensuniversity.manchester.ac.uk/interactives/history/egypt/

alabaster (AL-uh-bas-ter)—A fine-grained, usually white type of gypsum used for carving.

amulet (AM-yew-let)—A trinket or piece of jewelry worn as protection against evil.

archaeology (ARH-kee-uh-luh-gee)—The study of human history and prehistory by digging up sites and studying what is found.

artisan (AHR-ti-zen)—A worker who practices a trade or handicraft.

bureaucracy (byoor-AHK-ruh-see)—A group of government officials who follow rules and routines.

canal (KUH-nahl)—A manmade strip of water used for boats or irrigation.

cult—A system of religious worship directed toward a particular figure or object.

delta—A triangular deposit of rich soil at the mouth of a river.

economy (ee-KON-uh-mee)—Careful, thrifty management of resources, such as money, materials, or labor.

embalm—To treat a corpse with preservatives in order to prevent decay.

expedition (EX-puh-dih-shun)—A journey undertaken with a particular purpose by a group of people such as scientists or soldiers.

extensions (ek-STEN-shunz)—Pieces of real or fake hair that are attached to a person's head to add length or thickness to their own hair.

fertility (fur-TILL-uh-tee)—In a person, animal, or plant, the state of being able to conceive young or produce seeds.

harbor—A sheltered part of a body of water deep enough to provide anchorage for ships.

harem (HAHR-um)—A house or a section of a house reserved for females.

heretic (HER-uh-tik)—A person who holds controversial religious beliefs.

hypostyle (HY-puh-sti-yuhl)—Having a roof or ceiling supported by rows of columns.

ibis (EYE-biss)—A long-legged, wading bird.

incense (IN-sense)—A sweet-smelling substance, such as wood or plant gum, that is burned to produce a pleasant odor.

kohl (KOLE)—Powder used to darken the area around the eyes.

mercenary (MUHR-suh-neh-ree)—A professional soldier hired for service in an army in which the he has not been drafted to.

monotheistic (mah-noh-thee-IS-tik)—Believing that there is only one god.

mortuary (MOR-chu-ay-ree) **temple**—A temple for offerings and worship of a deceased person.

necropolis (neh-KRAW-poh-liss)—A cemetery, especially a large and elaborate one, in an ancient city.

negotiate (neh-GO-shee-ayt)—To arrange for or bring about through discussion and compromise.

obelisk (AW-buh-lisk)—A stone pillar with a square or rectangular shape that tapers toward the top, like a pyramid.

patron (PAY-truhn) **god**—A deity who protects a particular person, group of people, city, or country.

primeval (pri-MEE-vuhl)—Belonging to the earliest ages of the world.

procession (pruh-SEH-shun)—A group of people or things moving in an orderly and often ceremonial manner.

pylon—A monumental gateway featuring a pair of pyramids without pointy tops at the entrance of an ancient Egyptian temple.

reign (RAYN)—The period during which a monarch rules.

sanctuary (SANG-choo-ah-ree)—The holiest part of a sacred place.

shrine—A place where sacred relics are kept.

silt—A fine deposit of mud, clay, or soil, especially in a river or lake.

sphinx (SFINKS)—A figure in Egyptian myth having the body of a lion and the head of a human, ram, or hawk.

spoils—Plunder taken from an enemy in war or from a victim in robbery.

tomb (TOOM)—A vault or chamber for burial of the dead.

transcribe (tran-SKRYBE)—To write spoken words or thoughts on paper.

valley (VAL-ee)—An elongated lowland that usually contains a river.

vizier (VIZ-ee-uh)—In Ancient Egypt, the highest-ranking official to serve the pharaoh.